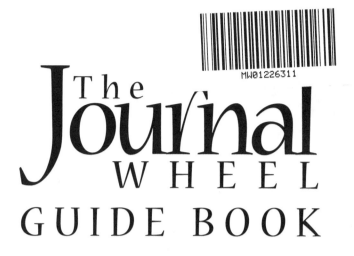

The Journal WHEEL
GUIDE BOOK

Set the wheel in motion for positive changes in your life.

By Deborah Bouziden

Rodgers & Nelsen
Publishing Co.
Loveland, Colorado

RNPub.com

We are always happy to hear from you. For questions or comments concerning the editorial content of this book, please write to: Rodgers & Nelsen Publishing Co., P.O. Box 7001, Loveland, CO 80537-0001

Look for other books published by Rodgers & Nelsen Publishing Co. wherever fine books are sold. For information visit us on the web: RNPub.com

First Edition February 2001

Printed in the United States of America

The Journal Wheel Guide Book is published by:

Rodgers & Nelsen Publishing Co.
P.O. Box 7001
Loveland, CO 80537-0001
970/593-9557

Production Credits:
Edited by Misty Lees, Kathryn Fanning
Cover, Layout, and Production by VW Design

Note from the Publisher

Congratulations for making the best decision you can make regarding your journaling and thank you for adding the *Journal Wheel* to your "tool box" of journaling items. Along with your pen (or pencil) and paper, think of this handy device as an integral part of your sessions. Use it as an idea generator, a way to move your thoughts along, a partner in your discovery of a subject, place or time.

This easy-to-use tool will promote and guide you to a nearly endless array of fascinating subjects and writing techniques. Using it will enhance your creativity and improve your writing and cognitive skills. Results will be evident sooner than you thought possible.

Finally, remember that journaling is a personal growth experience. The *Journal Wheel* was designed to enhance that experience.

We wish you much success in your life's journey and are glad RODGERS & NELSEN PUBLISHING is a small part of your trip.

Dedication

This book is dedicated to my grandmother, Rene Bruton,

who exhibits unconditional love on a daily basis;

my grandfather, Jesse Bruton, who, by example,

taught me how to tell family stories and preserve memories;

and to my friend and mentor, Kathryn Fanning,

who believes in me even when I don't believe in myself.

Table of Contents

Introduction

*"By writing down our thoughts, perceptions, and life
events today, we leave behind a priceless
legacy for future generations."*
–Deborah Bouziden

Journaling. No thanks, you may think. I'm not a writer. Neither was Anne Frank or are hundreds of other "journalists" who record their thoughts and feelings every day. The nice thing about journaling is you don't have to have perfect punctuation, create stunning sentences or know how to diagram them. All you have to do is put pen to paper.

Throughout history, mankind has learned and grown by the drawings and words left behind by ancestors. From cave wall stick figures to documents like the *Declaration of Independence,* we are who we are today because someone took the time to record events. As scientists have told us, what sets man apart from the animal kingdom is the ability to communicate with words, be they spoken or written.

If you *are* a writer, perhaps the thought of a journal breaks you out in a rash because you're afraid it's going to limit your other writing time. But did you know that journaling can enhance your creativity, increase productivity, and make you an overall *better* writer?

I started recording the events of my life in a diary when I was thirteen. Who would have believed I would be here, many years later, writing to you? Not me, that's for sure. I had plans to marry Elvis, become an attorney, and act on Broadway to thundering applause.

As I got older, I began recording my feelings and thoughts about my life's events. I have filled pages with interesting and mundane stories. Over the last few years, my writing has become more mature, solid, and fresh. On average, I spend fifteen to twenty minutes a day writing in my journal. Sometimes more, sometimes less. You may find ten minutes is enough for you or you may need longer. However much time you spend, remember, *that* time is for you. There are no rules except for the ones you designate.

Don't worry when it seems you have nothing to say. As I pulled out my old notebooks, locked diaries, and blank books, I found there were months, even a year, when I felt I had *nothing* to say. Who cared if I loved Elvis and Bucky Ryan at the same time? Who wanted to know about my dreams of making the world a better place? Why should the fact that I was scared on my wedding day and questioning my decision matter to anyone?

It shouldn't, but the further I read into the history of my life, the better *I* understood the person I am today. I find between the pages of my journal that I've recorded the friendships I've made, the career goals I've set and achieved, the relationships I've built and lost. Over the years my journal has become a close friend, a road map of where I've been and where I want to go. I have been able to confide anything to my journal without it judging me. I have written a dialogue with my mother about things I felt she did wrong when I was young; written a letter, which never will be mailed, to an old flame I'd like to see again; even listed fantasies I'm too timid to experience or share in *real* life. Even though my entries never will reach the celebrity of Anne Frank's (thank goodness) and won't be touted as great discoveries by historians, I know, for *me,* they have been cathartic and have provided a learning experience. Journal writing can do the same for you.

I know there are days when the most interesting thing in your life seems to be the weather. I've had them. We all have. The thing to do is write through those days, describe the weather if that's all there is. Perhaps that will be the key to unlocking a childhood memory like it did for me.

If you feel even the weather isn't worth writing about, allow me to offer some encouragement and suggestions. That's why I made the *Journal Wheel.* Granted, it probably won't make you the next William Shakespeare or foster love sonnets like Elizabeth Barrett Browning's, but that's not its purpose. Its function is to give you an idea of what to write about on those days when you can think of nothing.

The Journal Wheel is designed to give you a nudge, not a Tyson knockout blow. It is a creative tool for those interested in personal growth, development, and creative enhancement. It can be what you want it to be—a helping hand, a friend, or an encyclopedia of topics. And who knows? In the future as you read through your journal's pages, you might find, as I did, a "bard" inside you, after all.

How to Use the Wheel and Guide Book

"Our doubts are traitors,
And make us lose the good we oft might win
By fearing to attempt."
—William Shakespeare

It's easy to get started using the wheel. With all three disks turned toward you, line up the date with the month. Find what mood you're in and line that up with the month as well. At this point, date, month, and mood lines should be connected. Look in the technique window in the small wheel and you will see the technique chosen. Flip the wheel over and in the big window is the topic you will write about.

Close your eyes. Take three deep breaths. Remember, the technique and topic are meant to provide a starting point that can enhance your creativity and expand your writing experience. Don't feel pressured. This isn't supposed to imprison your thoughts. It's to set them free. Let those thoughts, impressions, feelings, and insights flow freely. With your eyes closed, what do you see in your mind? What do you feel about the chosen topic? Start writing.

Don't worry. The writing itself shouldn't overwhelm you. Start with ten to fifteen minutes a day. If you run over your time limit and become uncomfortable, set a timer next writing session.

What you write in need not be fancy. I've used spiral notebooks *and* the more expensive blank books. The words I read now don't sound any more special in the blank books than they do in the cheaper spirals. Use what feels comfortable to you. You are writing *your* life experiences, *your* thoughts, not someone else's.

Be sure to date your entries. Weeks, months, or even years from now, you'll be able to look back and see what was happening in your life and when. In the future, after you are gone, it will be an excellent reference source for your relatives or may perhaps alert other readers to some historical significance.

The wheel can be used for years to come. It has as many different combinations as there are days in the month and moods you experience. The key is not to feel you have to use it every day, but use it when you need it to assist you with journal entries. Make it a game; make it fun and grow with the process of discovering what's inside you.

This book is designed to guide you through descriptions of the techniques as well as point out suggested topics and the way to write them, but *you* will have to find the treasure in your own life's museum.

After you have found your daily writing topic on the wheel, go to the TECHNIQUE section of this book (page 5). Some techniques are self-explanatory. Others may require reading through their paragraphs a couple of times to understand the power of their procedures.

The THIRTY-ONE TOPICS listed (starting on page 12) are to give you a starting point. Some days you will turn the wheel, see the topic, and know immediately what you want, need, and are going to write about. Other days, you may need more help. Go to the chosen topic page, look over the suggestions, and see if anything grabs your attention. When you discover your topic, start writing.

Another section you may find helpful is EXTRA TOPICS (page 44). These are sentence starters. You may want to use them alone or in combination with a technique. For instance, if your technique is "List" and you find a sentence starter that begins "I really want to ...", make a list of things you want or have to do.

You will find the more you use the *Journal Wheel,* the less dependent you will be on the book. That is how it should be. Read it and use it when you need it. And remember, the book is small. It's not to be studied. It's to help you write and record pieces of your life. So let's get started.

Techniques

"The significant problems we face cannot be solved at the same level of thinking we were at when we created them."

-Albert Einstein

While there are no set rules about how to write entries in your journal, here are some of the most popular techniques and the ones used on the *Journal Wheel*. Books like Kathleen Adams' *Journal to the Self*, Sheila Bender's *A Year in the Life*, Louise DeSalvo's *Writing As A Way Of Healing*, and Dr. Ira Progoff's *At A Journal Workshop* go into greater depth about journaling techniques and give examples of many. Use them if they help. If you have read other books with similar methods that work for you, go with them. Remember, these are *your* writings, *your* journals. Now, for your consideration, here are some recommended techniques.

Character Sketch-

The character sketch is a great vehicle for seeing ourselves as others see us and for giving us *new* views on people and things around us. A character sketch is a written description of an individual, a personified object, or yourself. While using this technique, you want to describe not only the tangible features of your subject, but the intangible as well. Pretend you are an investigator. What do you see about the person or thing that others should be aware of? What secrets can you uncover about them? As a twist, imagine you are someone else; write how they would see you. If you are having difficulty in a relationship, project yourself into the other person's position and describe yourself from that viewpoint. Seeing yourself from another's vantage point is like looking in a mirror. Reality stares you in the face. You will be amazed what you can discover.

> **SKILL BUILDER:** *Using this technique will help you build and identify characters in your stories.*

Clustering- Clustering is known to work both sides of the brain; the right is allowed to create while the left is allowed to organize or structure. Writers have used clustering for years to get story ideas down on paper. Businessmen use clustering to brainstorm projects or to manage them. This process is also described as webbing, mind mapping, or bubbling. Clustering is the process of choosing a key word or phrase, putting it in the middle of a blank sheet of paper, circling or boxing it, and using free association to come up with another word that relates to it. Write down the next word that comes to mind and draw a line connecting it to the one before. Continue to work outward until you can think of no more words to connect. When finished, study your cluster. What patterns do you see? What similarities? Differences? Maybe there is one word that interests you more than others. Write it down and work through the process again.

SKILL BUILDER: Use this technique when you are brainstorming article or book ideas and searching for marketing considerations.

Dialogue- The dialogue technique is valuable because it can provide greater insight to your life by letting your subconscious view yourself as another person would. "Within each of us is an underground stream of images and recollections that is nothing more or less than our interior life," Dr. Ira Progoff said in *Psychology Today,* March 1981. That stream can manifest itself as we write dialogues. A dialogue is a written conversation between you and someone or something else. The unique part about this technique is that you play both parts. You may feel uncomfortable at first, but work through one set and you will find it is worth the anxiety. It is set up in form similar to a film script. On a blank page, write your name followed by a semicolon. Begin by asking a question of the subject of your dialog. Jot down that person's or thing's name, add a semicolon and wait for an answer. Even though you are in both roles, you will be surprised at the things that come to mind. You don't always have to ask questions. Make observations, then listen for your inner voice to answer you. You can dialogue with relatives (living or dead), friends, enemies, your conscience, current affairs, money, even God. You set the limits.

SKILL BUILDER: This technique will strengthen your fiction and non-fiction dialogue skills. Listen to your characters. Let them talk to you. Then, write down what they say.

Dreams (or Dream Analysis)-

Writing down your dreams can show patterns or perhaps explain the reason you act or react to certain situations. A dream (day or night) can be described as a sequence of sensations, images, thoughts, etc., a fanciful vision of the conscious mind, a state of abstraction or reverie. You can discover vast amounts about your inner thoughts by recording your night dreams, but don't limit yourself. Write about daydreams, too. If you are recording night dreams, jot down not only the contents of the dream, but any symbols you may have noticed, recurrences (repetitious scenes from previous dreams), whether the dream was in black and white, and what *you* think the dream meant. Jotting down all the facets of these "mind movies" may help you uncover hidden agendas even you weren't aware of. There are several books you can purchase that will guide you through interpreting your dreams. Don't become legalistic with the process. Relax. If your subconscious has something to tell you, it will. If you choose to write about your daydreams, be as specific as you are with your nighttime dreams. Jot down why and how the daydream has distracted you. Do you have the same one over and over? Are they connected with events in your life, goals, or relationship problems? Write down what your mind is telling you. Perhaps you'll find solutions or new avenues of personal growth.

SKILL BUILDER: Studying your dreams will help you build depth in your story characters. When you begin to understand yourself, you can understand others.

Freewriting-

Freewriting is exactly that. You write about whatever comes to mind for a given length of time. You write continuously, never stopping no matter what you write. Don't worry about grammar, punctuation, or spelling in these writings. The key is to keep your hand moving across the page. As long as you are writing, this technique will open the doors of your mind, allow thoughts to flow. You may find yourself switching subjects in mid-sentence. That's okay. Flow where your subconscious wants to take you. You may want to put yourself in a certain situation and write about how you deal with it. Guided imagery is good to experiment with when you are freewriting. We won't delve into guided imagery here, but several of the books listed in the RECOMMENDED READING chapter do.

SKILL BUILDER: Freewriting can help you manage and control story plots and article ideas when they flood into your head. Set a timer and let them flow onto paper.

Life Snapshots-

This technique can best be described as writing still pictures of your life. After you have film developed, you hold the photos in your hand, study them, and sometimes describe them to others. That's what you do with this process. Snapshots help you see your life's events in a fresh way. They help you gain insight by viewing the details of a particular and specific time. Think of one event in your life, stop the motion and write everything you see in your mind's eye. Record what you are wearing. What do you hear? Smell? How do you feel? Excited? Scared? Content? Are you touching something? Someone? What are you looking at? What is around you? Who is around you? What are you doing? What are others doing? Are you alone? Be sure to include details of objects in your description as well. Like symbols in your dreams, these items may have a meaning.

SKILL BUILDER: This technique will strengthen your narrative skills. The more observant you are of the world around you and the better you can describe those observations, the clearer you will communicate on paper.

Lists-

Lists are just that. Lists. They are good for keeping inventory and, like freewriting, can allow thoughts to flow more smoothly. With this technique, you start with a topic and a blank sheet of paper, then begin writing single words or short phrases pertaining to the topic. The list can be as short as three items or as long as a hundred. There is no number limit. The process is excellent for recording items in your home, making out an invitation list for a party, counting your blessings and your friends, or setting goals. You can set a time limit for this exercise or let your thoughts carry you from one item to another. Like clustering, write as long as words present themselves to you.

SKILL BUILDER: Use this technique to write down lists of article ideas, points you want to make in an article, experts you want to contact, or steps you need to take to get a project in the mail.

Poetry or Drawing-

I once heard poetry described as "Word Painting." With this technique, you can be creative with words, colors, markers, or paints. Your only limitation is your imagination. This technique is meant to be fun. As you relax and work

8

with different mediums, you will find a fresher approach to creativity. You can write a poem—long, short, rhymed, unrhymed, structured or unstructured—or grab whatever color medium you have available, head to a blank sheet of paper and draw, paint, or color. Who says a journal has to be filled with words? Open any older journal and you will find sketches of trees, people and animals, as well as unrecognizable items. Drawings, good or bad, are a means of expression. Remember, you are trying to invite your creative muse.

Perhaps you shudder at the thought of writing poetry, but you can express yourself in this medium as well. If you are not inclined to haiku, couplets, or epigrams, try the acrostic. Go back to when you were in grade school. Remember, the acrostic poem was based on the premise of taking a word, any word, and writing the word down the length of the page, using one letter per line. Each letter then gets a word or phrase to flow with the theme of the main word until all the letters are used. For instance, an acrostic on "journaling" might read like this: Joining Otherwise Useless Ramblings Never Allowing Language's Intimate Nefarious Grumblings OR Journey Opportunity Understanding Release Notation Analyze Label Introspection Novice Gratifying.

SKILL BUILDER: *Using the poetry or drawing process will allow you to have fun with words, shapes, and colors. By relaxing your mind and allowing yourself to create, you stimulate the right side of your brain, giving it permission to be inventive.*

Road Maps-

With this technique, you will record significant moments or particular points in your life. Consider them road signs. When you travel you look at the road signs for clues to your destination. In your life you will take many journeys. Just as you return to some of the same places time and again, writing down your life's "road maps" allows you to see patterns and roads you have taken, paths harmful or helpful. "Road maps" are generally short phrases written in a list format. Keep phrases simple and to the point. You can start with an overview of your life. For instance, use the opening phrase, "I was born." Then ask yourself, "What happened next?" You might write something like, "my mom died" or "we moved." What happened next? "I made a new friend." "I started school." You get the point. You are looking at the road signs of your life. Another place to start would be "It was a time

when …", or "I started …", or "In the beginning …".
Review your road maps often. Look for things that have
changed and things that have remained the same as patterns.
Just as scenes along the road change from season to season,
you will notice different views of your life. Keep moving.
You've not reached your destination yet.

SKILL BUILDER: You can use this technique to map out your fictional characters' lives or your writing career.

Summaries-

This process allows you to summarize the events of your
life. Summarizing can give you a measuring stick to see how
you've grown or how you've stagnated. It can encourage you
when you see goals reached or spur you onward when you
see how close you came.

In these writings, you will tell what happened. Such
summaries can range from a paragraph to as long as you
want. Express your feelings, describe places or events, tell
what you learned or enjoyed. Summaries can be written on
any subject—vacations, projects you're working on, relationships, cities you've visited, whatever you are experiencing.

Looking back over the past week, write a page, two, or
even three that encapsulate what has happened to you. Now
go farther back, a month. Do the same thing. Check back a
year. You may want to summarize seasons, comparing them
to how your life has changed.

These summaries don't have to be outward summaries
only. For instance, you might have lost thirty pounds, but the
confidence you have gained in yourself may be more
important.

SKILL BUILDER: Use this technique to summarize conferences and workshops you attend. Write down who you met, important contacts you may have made, what advice you received (if any). This information may be valuable as you grow in your career.

Unsent Letters-

Unsent letters express anger, hurt, resentment, or other
negative emotions. They also can be used to vent feelings
you don't feel allowed to express in society or to brag about
the accomplishments in your life. They are written from a
one-sided perspective—yours. Since no one will read your
letter, express feelings in any form or fashion. Do you have
something you've never had the chance to tell someone?

Angry with your boss, but know if you told him off, you'd lose your job? Need to let off some steam? Write a letter, as long as you'd like, as filled with love, anger, remorse, as you need it to be. The key to the unsent letter is that you're not going to mail it. Visualize for whom the letter is meant and let your feelings flow onto the paper. Don't censor yourself. This is your chance to tell the person or object what you feel needs to be expressed. When finished, if you feel uncomfortable leaving it in your journal, make a ritual by tearing it up or burning it.

SKILL BUILDER: When you receive a rejection slip from an editor, use this technique to vent disappointment or irritation. If society is running its fingernails over the chalkboard of your life, perhaps a heated "Letter To The Editor" is in order. After careful editing, you might want to mail this one to your local paper.

Views-

The Views technique is where you look back at the choices you've made, the way you live your life, or some decision you are in the process of making now, then write about how your life would be different if you chose the alternative. You know the old adage, "Hindsight is 20/20." This technique may point out the flaws if you had chosen differently and prove your decision was the right one for you. It can give you a clearer understanding of your relationships with others. For instance, ask yourself, what if I had chosen to marry Bob? How would my life be different? Perhaps you'd have children. Perhaps you wouldn't. By looking at your life from different viewpoints, this technique can help you make better decisions and live a more fulfilled life.

SKILL BUILDER: This technique will help when you are deciding which projects to work on, what markets to approach, and how to spend your working days. Write down what would happen in each of the situations. For instance, what will happen to your career if you go with an agent in New York? On the flip side, what will happen if you go with one in Kansas?

Wildcard-

Choose any of the previous twelve techniques at random and use that technique.

Thirty-One Topics

"Destiny is not a matter of chance,
it is a matter of choice;
it is not a thing to be waited for,
it is a thing to be achieved."
—William Jennings Bryan

In this chapter, you will find ideas and suggestions for using the techniques with the topic list. You don't have to take these suggestions. If you read through the lists and find an idea is sparked, by all means go with it. These are only meant to prime the writing pump.

This chapter is not to be read as you would read a novel. It's to be used as you would a dictionary. Topics and techniques are listed alphabetically for easy access. Find the topic and then look for the technique listed as a subtopic.

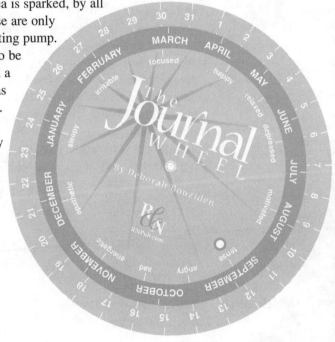

The Arts

Character Sketch- Have you seen a movie or play whose characters made such an impression you've remembered them for a long time? Write about a character from a play, television show, movie or book; or personify a statue or other inanimate object.

Clustering- Write a cluster about movies you've seen, books you've read, artists you admire or paintings you own.

Dialogue- Have you wanted to join a theatre group, talk to a celebrity or political activist, or converse with a dead poet? Now is your chance to hear what they might say in a dialogue with you.

Dreams- Jot down a dream relating to the arts. Have you ever dreamed you acted on stage, painted, sculpted, or traveled abroad? If not, have you ever daydreamed about those activities?

Freewriting- Write about an artist, actor/actress, or musician you admire. What are his or her best qualities? Would you like to be that person? Why or why not?

Life Snapshots- Write down a "snapshot" of a concert you've attended, a scene from a movie, or an interview with a celebrity.

Lists- List movies you have seen that you enjoyed or upcoming shows you'd like to see. List your favorite chefs, talk show hosts, artists, etc.

Poetry- "Word-paint" or draw your favorite musical artists. Put on a CD and let your creativity flow.

Road Maps- Have you crossed paths with a painter, writer, political figure, or celebrity you admire? Write about your experience starting with "I went …".

Summaries- Write about an artistic experience you had, whether attending a gallery opening or an outdoor arts festival. Do you cross-stitch, sculpt, or make candles? Describe your experience and how you feel about the creative process.

Unsent Letters- Write a letter to an artist you admire. Tell him why you admire his work. Mention that you'd like to meet him and explain why.

Views- How do you feel about the latest movie you saw? What impressed you with the painting you purchased? What is special about the art you admire? Write down your opinions.

Blessings

Character Sketch- Write a sketch about the people or things you are thankful for. Describe their best attributes.

Clustering- Start with your significant other, a friend, or your parents and add people who have come into your life and blessed it in a significant way. You also can cluster items or attributes you are blessed with.

Dialogue- Have a dialogue with God, an angel, or Mary, the Mother of Jesus. If a special friend has blessed you by being there when times are tough, dialogue with that friend.

Dreams- Have you dreamed something would happen and it came true? Did you see that dream as a blessing? If so, write about it. Do you consider your dreams blessings in general?

Freewriting- Write about the greatest blessing in your life—husband, children, parents, friends, or career.

Life Snapshots- Consider a time in your work, family life, or personal life when you have felt content. Write about it.

Lists- List the times and incidents when you have had favor with the government, family or friends, or had experiences in good health.

Poetry- Try an acrostic with the word "blessings." Go through photographs and make a collage of the things you have been blessed with in your life.

Road Maps- Write down the road maps (analyze and think about how one thing led to another) for blessings you have enjoyed at work, or in your personal or family life.

Summaries- Write a paragraph of thanks for good times, things or incidents in your life.

Unsent Letters- Write letters or notes to people who have brightened your day. Perhaps you don't know the person's name who smiled and gave you encouragement on a rough day, but write and say thanks.

Views- Do you feel you are blessed? In what ways? If you don't feel blessed, why not?

Childhood Memories

Character Sketch- Write about a special childhood friend—a person, stuffed animal, or pet.

Clustering- Make a cluster about your earliest memory—birthday party, traumatic event, loss, or first day of school.

Dialogue- Have a dialogue with your childhood pet, a long lost friend you'd like to see again, a favorite toy, or a childhood home.

Dreams- Have you suffered from nightmares that have recurred through time? Do you have dreams which take you back to your childhood? Write about them.

Freewriting- What troubles you about your childhood? What did you enjoy? Choose one incident and write how you would change things if you could or why you wouldn't change them.

Life Snapshots- Revisit an incident or place of your childhood. Did you swim in the river, play in a park, ride a pony?

Lists- Make a list of favorite toys, friends, celebrations. You can use this list for clustering ideas later.

Poetry- Do you remember a poem, nursery rhyme, or fairy tale learned when you were a child? Write it down. Pull out the markers, crayons, or colored pencils. Draw a scribble, then color it in.

Road Maps- Start at a particular point in time (first grade, second grade, etc.) and write maps about your life's progression. Road maps are perfect for childhood memories.

Summaries- Possible summary topics: a childhood illness, broken bones, missed school activities, awards. Tell how these affected you later in life.

Unsent Letters- Write a letter to friends you've lost track of, celebrities you've wanted to meet since childhood, or individuals you admired from afar but were too afraid to approach.

Views- Do you think your parents did a good job of raising you? Did you receive a quality education? Was your family welcomed into the community or ostracized? Write about why you think this was.

Community Service

Character Sketch- Choose a civic leader, outstanding community member, or your next door neighbor and describe.

Clustering- Consider a community service project like building a park for kids, city beautification, or highway trash clean-up; cluster ideas and ways to expand or complete these projects.

Dialogue- Share a dialogue with an irate neighbor. Pretend you're at a city council meeting speaking on a topic that you are passionate about. Dialogue with the mayor, a policeman, or the trash collector.

Dreams- Have you ever dreamed you were in another town? Ever daydreamed about something you could do to benefit our planet? Write it down.

Freewriting- Write about the homeless people in your community, another problem your community faces, or the irritation you experience from road detours or rude drivers.

Life Snapshots- Jot down your first experience voting. See yourself going into the polling booth and casting your vote. Have you volunteered at the American Red Cross, given clothes or appliances to Goodwill, or manned a phone booth for a charity event? Write about that experience.

Lists- Make a list of ways you can help in your neighborhood, city, or state.

Poetry- Take the name of your city or state and write an acrostic poem (see p. 9 for an example). Write free verse about a vacation spot near you. Draw a map of your neighborhood or city.

Road Maps- Write about when you moved into your neighborhood. You also can write a road map about your experiences around town.

Summaries- Summarize trips into your city, community service time, or experiences at your local post office.

Unsent Letters- Write a letter to the editor of your local paper. Sound off to the mayor or a city councilman.

Views- How do you view your community? Do you think there could be more local interaction between neighbors? Do you feel more people should become involved in community projects?

Completions

Character Sketch- Personify a project you have completed in the last month. It can be anything from a cooked meal to you stopping smoking. Write a sketch describing your project.

Clustering- Start with something you want to do; cluster steps you can take to complete the task.

Dialogue- Write a dialogue between you and a project, mentor, or adversary.

Dreams- Have you ever finished a dream? Write about it. If you were the Sandman, what dreams would you allow people to experience? Write down a dream you've always wanted to have.

Freewriting- Freewrite about projects you'd like to complete this week, this month, or this year. Perhaps you have a lifelong project you'd like to do. Choose one and write about it.

Life Snapshots- Think about projects you have completed. Write about one of the moments when you finished, before you put away your supplies.

Lists- Make a list of projects you have completed. Focus on certain areas of your life or certain time periods. You also can list the steps you took in completing a project.

Poetry- Choose a poetry form and in one sitting, write a poem. If you prefer to draw, paint, or color, complete the project from start to finish.

Road Maps- Think about how you completed a project from point A to point B. In one sentence stroke, write a road map as to how you did it.

Summaries- Summarize a project in one or two paragraphs. Don't give all the details, just write an overview.

Unsent Letters- Write a letter to someone who helped you along the way or someone who discouraged you. Perhaps you need to write a letter to someone who is gone from your life now.

Views- Write about how you feel when you start a new project, when you get in the middle of one, or when you finish.

Education

Character Sketch- Write a sketch about an admired teacher in grade school, high school or college. Was there an instructor you didn't care for? You might want to write about that person.

Clustering- Choose a subject or class and cluster what you learned in that class. You may want to want to cluster your graduating class and see how many names you can remember.

Dialogue- You can dialogue with friends, teachers, school administrators, or subjects. Topics here are endless.

Dreams- Write about dreams you had in school. Do you remember daydreaming in class? What did you think about? Were you ever caught and punished?

Freewriting- Possible subjects: classes you liked, extracurricular activities, or embarrassing moments.

Life Snapshots- Freeze-frame the night you graduated. Perhaps something humiliating happened to you. Remember the first time you fell in love. Write about one of these moments.

Lists- List your friends, books you read, classes you took, teachers' names, and so on.

Poetry- Write a poem about your school, your first love, the first day of school, or the last. Take your class motto and build a poem on its concept. Remember, we're also considering drawing as "Poetry," so roughly sketch your school building. Draw a blueprint of the inside or maybe one of your childhood homes.

Road Maps- Write a road map of how you progressed through a school year. Another map suggestion is an activity you were involved in.

Summaries- Summarize a particular year of school: first grade, second grade, third grade, etc.

Unsent Letters- Write a letter to a friend you've lost track of, a secret love, a teacher you admired, a teacher you despised. You also can write a letter to today's board of education detailing what's wrong with the school system.

Views- Do you think you received a quality education? Do you think it cost too much? Write about how you would improve today's educational system or what you feel you could have done to improve your own education.

Entertainment

Character Sketch- Think of a comedian, actor, sports figure, your son, your daughter, your pet, anyone or anything that entertains you. Write about one.

Clustering- Choose a subject like books and write a cluster of all your favorite books. You can do the same with movies, sports venues, hobbies, etc.

Dialogue- Write a dialogue with a cartoon character. Try taking your favorite movie, changing the dialogue in a scene and then have a conversation with the movie's main character.

Dreams- Finish one of your dreams by writing the end of it. Write about the symbols you remember in your dreams. Do you remember your friends telling you about their dreams? Write down what you remember.

Freewriting- Write about anything that entertains you. It may be reading a book, watching a ball game on television, playing tennis, or simply watching a honeybee sip nectar from a flower.

Life Snapshots- Write about a time when you entertained others. Have you had guests over for dinner? Are you a speaker? Do you Sing? Play a sport? Teach?

Lists- Jot down things that entertain you in various areas of your life. Write a list of things that may entertain children, elderly people, or pets.

Poetry- Write a Dr. Seuss-style poem. Read it to your family. Print outlines from the internet or color in your own collection of coloring books.

Road Maps- What do you find yourself doing or watching at numerous times? Write a road map as to how you became involved with a particular type of entertainment.

Summaries- Choose a form of entertainment you enjoy and summarize it in one or two paragraphs.

Unsent Letters- Write a letter to someone who you admire in the entertainment field. It can be a singer, athlete, celebrity, agent, etc. Is there something that person does that you feel you could do better?

Views- How would you define entertainment? What would you change about the media and its feeding frenzy on celebrities? Or would you change anything?

Family

Character Sketch- Write a sketch about your brother, sister, son, daughter, cousin, aunt, uncle, or significant other.

Clustering- Work on your family tree. Starting with your grandparents, fill your cluster with family members' names.

Dialogue- Dialogue with a family member: brother, cousin, second cousin, etc.

Dreams- Write down a dream when one or more family members have been involved. If one has never been in your dreams, write down why you think that's so.

Freewriting- Write anything at all about your family. Are you close? Why or why not? Do you still see your cousins? How well do you know your second and third cousins? Are there any "black sheep" in your family?

Life Snapshots- Think about your family gatherings. Choose one and write about what you were wearing, what you were doing. What was the occasion? How many family members were there?

Lists- List the many occupations your family members have had. List the names of cousins, aunts, uncles, etc. List the different parts of the country they live in, those who went to college, or special talents family members exhibit.

Poetry- Take your last name and write a poem about it. It can be any shape or form.

Road Maps- Write a road map about your family's history. You can write about your immediate family, past generations, or how you link with second and third generations.

Summaries- Summarize time spent with family members. Write about family reunions, holidays, or funerals.

Unsent Letters- Write letters to family members who may have made you angry and to whom you didn't feel free to express your opinion at that time. Write letters to cousins, aunts, and uncles you may have lost track of or those who have passed away.

Views- What is your view of your family? Do you think family ties could be stronger? Write your opinions on family life.

Food

Character Sketch- Write a sketch about your favorite food. You also can sketch your favorite cook, be it your mom, dad, Emeril Lagasse, or Martha Stewart.

Clustering- Take one food item and cluster the many ways you can eat it, other foods or wines that can be served with it, or those ingredients you might need to make it.

Dialogue- Have a dialogue with food groups, individual foods, specific drinks, or great chefs.

Dreams- Have you ever dreamed of food? What do you think food dreams mean? Do you think there is any validity to having nightmares after eating certain foods? Why?

Freewriting- Write whatever you want, as long as the subject pertains to food. Have you dieted all your life? Do you eat to live or live to eat? Is food not a problem for you?

Life Snapshots- Think back to a meal. Write a snapshot about why it was memorable. Write about a meal you ate today.

Lists- Write down your favorite recipes or your favorite menus.

Poetry- Write a poem about your favorite fruit or vegetable. Include sensory details like texture, taste, and aroma. Make a macaroni collage, construct a spaghetti or toothpick building, or decorate a cake with different shaped candies.

Road Maps- Write about how you came to like or dislike a certain food. If you are struggling with your weight, write a road map on how you came to be where you are on the scale. If your weight is perfect, explain how you arrived there.

Summaries- Summarize your favorite meals, snacks, desserts. How do you make them? These summaries could be similar to directions in a cookbook. You can summarize family feasts, travel foods, or lunches for work or school.

Unsent Letters- Write a letter to your local grocer, the owner of your favorite restaurant, or a farmer. Mention what you like or dislike.

Views- What are your overall views on food? Do you think the government allows too many preservatives? How do you suggest we handle the labeling issue? Do you like fresh fruits and vegetables, canned or frozen?

Friends

Character Sketch- Write a sketch about one of your friends. Perhaps you consider your car or pet a friend. Write about it.

Clustering- Divide your life into sections and list friends in each: work, private life, etc.

Dialogue- Has a friend done something that really made you angry? Have you wanted to talk to one of your friends about something, but haven't? Now is your chance.

Dreams- What are some of your dreams and those of your friends? Do any of them include your other friends? What are your daydreams?

Freewriting- Write about what you and your friends do together. Choose one or the whole group. Write about your best friend, your most loyal, or a false friend.

Life Snapshots- Choose a specific time or a segment of time when you were with a friend and write about it. Did you attend a class together, an event, or just go out to dinner and a movie? You also might want to consider writing about the moment when you might go your separate ways.

Lists- List your friends. List why they are important to you. List their occupations.

Poetry- Write a poem about an individual friend or the group as a whole. Make a collage with pictures you have collected through the friendship.

Road Maps- Choose a friendship and write about how it came into being. Have you had estrangements from friends? Write a map about that.

Summaries- Choose one of your friends and summarize your relationship. Has your friend always been supportive? What do you have in common? Have you ever disagreed? Summarize what the disagreement was about and how you worked through it.

Unsent Letters- Has a friend ever embarrassed you? Made you mad? From telling your friend to shape up to complaining about table manners, clothing choices, or your friend's latest true love, now is your chance. Write your friend a letter expressing your feelings on issues that have been bothering you.

Views- What do you consider true friendship? Do you think friends should be given second chances when they betray the friendship? How do you think a friendship should grow? If one of your friends broke the law, would you turn her in?

Frustrations

Character Sketch- Give form to your frustrations. Write a detailed sketch of one. If it did have a form, what would it look like, where would it live, and how would it act? You also can write sketches about people who cause you frustration.

Clustering- Write down a word related to a particular frustration, person or situation in the middle of a blank sheet of paper. Cluster ways to relieve the frustration. Add certain situations and times to see if there is a pattern.

Dialogue- Dialogue with people, situations, or experiences. Write out your frustrations and try to work through them.

Dreams- Write about a frustrating dream. Maybe it's one that keeps recurring or one whose meaning escapes you. Perhaps it's a nightmare you can't get out of your mind.

Freewriting- Is there something in your life now that frustrates you? Perhaps you want to lose weight, get married, get a divorce, have children, solve financial problems, start a business, or leave your current job.

Life Snapshots- Think back to a time when you felt frustrated. It could have been a traffic tie-up, lack of money, or maybe you were lost. Put yourself back into the situation and write about how you felt in the moment.

Lists- Write a list of your frustrations. Work from a category. List frustrations with your finances, family, or personal life.

Poetry- Identify a particular frustration, write down the word and work out an acrostic poem. Using a black crayon, draw a picture of what your problem might look like. When finished, wad up the paper and throw it away.

Road Maps- If your frustrations stem from finances, write a life map about how you arrived at this particular crossroad. If they are from health, weight, or relationship difficulties, do the same.

Summaries- Choose a current frustration and summarize it. How did it start? What and who does it involve? How do you plan to resolve it?

Unsent Letters- Write a letter to the person who frustrates you, be it the president, a city councilman, your neighbor, or your spouse. You also can write letters to groups of people like employees of the Internal Revenue Service.

Views- How do you deal with frustration? Do you become annoyed at people who can't deal with their own frustrations? Give your view on one of these topics.

Goals

Character Sketch- Personify your goals and write a sketch about one of them. Has there been someone who has helped you reach your goal? Write a sketch about the person who inspired you.

Clustering- Write down a goal in the center of a sheet of paper. Cluster ideas as to how you will reach this goal. Remember, these goals can be daily or lifetime, short-term or long-term.

Dialogue- Dialogue with one of your goals, a supporter, or a person who didn't believe in you.

Dreams- Have you daydreamed about your goals and worked out how you would reach them? Write down what you visualized.

Freewriting- Write about your daily, weekly, monthly, yearly, 5-year, or 10-year goals.

Life Snapshots- Choose one time when you achieved a goal and write how you felt the moment you reached it. Choose a time when you knew you had failed to reach your goal.

Lists- Make a list of your goals—short-term, mid-term, or long-term. You can make a daily, monthly, yearly, or lifetime list.

Poetry- Write a short rhyme about goals. Try a humorous poem. Draw a picture using stick figures on how you reached your goal. Make an inspirational poster with pictures and words cut from magazines to help focus on your goal.

Road Maps- Choose one achievement and write a map on how you accomplished it. Write about reaching a personal goal. Next, write about a business goal.

Summaries- Choose either your personal or business goals and write a summary about each one. What is your strategy? What will you do if you fail? What will you do if you succeed?

Unsent Letters- Write a letter to someone who was supportive or helped you reach your goal. Write a letter to the person who was skeptical.

Views- What is your view on goal setting? Do you see it as an integral part to getting what you want? Do you think goals are a help or hindrance? Write your view on the goal process.

Hobbies & Crafts

Character Sketch- Choose a specific hobby or craft that you enjoy. Think about an expert in the field and describe in a sketch.

Clustering- Write the name of a hobby or craft in the center of a sheet of paper. Cluster out supplies you need to buy, directions, or classes you need to take.

Dialogue- Dialogue with Martha Stewart or another guru in your hobby field. If you are facing problems with a craft you are working on, dialogue with your subconscious; see if you can't find an answer to your problem.

Dreams- Write down any symbols you may have in your dreams. As a hobby, try finding what's behind those symbols. Look up their meaning in a book about dreams and analyze their significance to you in particular.

Freewriting- Write down ideas you may have for hobby or craft projects. Is there a hobby you would like to take up, but feel you're not talented enough or don't have enough time?

Life Snapshots- Remember when you were working on a project. Snap a mental picture and write about what you are doing.

Lists- Make a list of hobbies or crafts you would like to do. Take one and make a list of things you need to purchase, techniques you need to learn, and what you will accomplish.

Poetry- Invent a puppet character. Have him write a poem about being a puppet. Make a notebook to hold your poetry. Paint or decorate the outside cover.

Road Maps- Starting with "I want(ed) to …", write a map about a craft project you want to start and complete, or one you have completed.

Summaries- Choose one of your hobby or craft projects and summarize how you completed it. If you are just starting a project, summarize how you will follow through to the end.

Unsent Letters- Have you started a complicated project you couldn't finish? Write a letter to the person who gave the instructions. Try writing a letter to a craft magazine or a local television station praising coverage of hobbies and crafts you enjoy or explain what you find disturbing about that coverage.

Views- Do you like hobbies and crafts? Do you think they help relieve stress? Should you turn a hobby into a business? Write your views on craft stores, classes, or hobbies and crafts your family participates in.

Health

Character Sketch- Pretend you are someone else and write a sketch about yourself. Write a sketch about someone you think has the perfect body, or yourself with the perfect body.

Clustering- Choose a word from the following list: alternative medicine, diet, exercise, stress reduction, habits, rest. Use one as your focal point and cluster how you can improve in these areas.

Dialogue- Dialogue with your health care professional, your subconscious on how to have the perfect you, or your inner critic.

Dreams- Write about a dream when you exerted physical energy. Maybe you were running, swimming, participating in sexual activity. Do you daydream about having the perfect body?

Freewriting- Are there things in your current lifestyle you'd like to change that would make your health better? Have you discovered tips or shortcuts that help you concentrate on being healthier? What do you think about alternative medicine? Choose a topic on health, yours or public health in general, and write about it.

Life Snapshots- Look at a moment in time when you were doing something physical. Write about that fraction of time. You also can write on times when you were eating nutritional food, had high self-esteem, or loathed yourself.

Lists- List your goals for a healthy lifestyle.

Poetry- Choose a health topic like AIDS, cancer, diabetes, or heart disease and write a poem about it or someone you know who suffers from an affliction. Draw a food pyramid, heart-healthy diagram, or poster on the dangers of smoking.

Road Maps- Choose a time in your life when you felt good about yourself. Write a map about the things you were doing, programs you were following, etc. You also may choose a time when you weren't feeling so well.

Summaries- Summarize your health or lifestyle over the past one, five, or ten years.

Unsent Letters- Do you know someone who needs to change his or her lifestyle? Is there someone who has made an impact on the way you live your life? Do you exercise every day with a fitness guru and would like to let him know how much you enjoy the time? Write a letter to that person.

Views- What are your views on health or health-related issues? Does the government do enough to control infectious diseases? How would you improve our current health care system?

Image/Appearance

Character Sketch- Write a sketch about a male or female whose appearance is striking. They don't have to be outwardly beautiful. Maybe it's their self-confidence, their boldness that you admire. Write about it. Write a sketch about the image you would like to portray.

Clustering- Take attributes you would like to exhibit in your image or appearance and cluster from them. Topics can include self-confidence, bravery, or gracefulness, to name a few.

Dialogue- Write a dialogue with your inner self, your confidence, the bathroom scale, or mirror. Discuss ways in which they help or hinder the way you feel about yourself.

Dreams- In your dreams, how do you act? Write about a dream where you were self-confident, afraid, or shy. You also can choose any other attribute related to your dreams and write about that.

Freewriting- Think about the way people dress. Write about another person's clothing style. Write about yours. What do you think the clothes people choose say about them?

Life Snapshots- Write about a time when you felt sure of yourself, when you felt self-conscious or out of place.

Lists- Make a list of your attributes or ones you'd like to exhibit. What qualities do you admire in others?

Poetry- Write a poem about a celebrity you admire, traits and qualities you inherited from your parents, or a child's boldness and curiosity. Go through magazines, cut out pictures and make a collage of hairstyles you'd like to experiment with. Cut out or draw an outfit you'd like to wear.

Road Maps- Are you confident, timid, self-motivated, a leader? Write a map on how you arrived at a certain place. You may be a leader at work, but timid and shy in building relationships.

Summaries- Think about your attributes. Choose one and summarize its qualities and/or drawbacks.

Unsent Letters- Write a letter to someone you admire or perhaps someone you loathe. Tell the person why you feel the way you do.

Views- Do you think people should be judged by their appearance? Why do you think most people judge others by the way they look and dress? Do you feel image is important? If so, why? If not, why not?

Inventory of Life, Possessions, Etc.

Character Sketch- Write a sketch about a person in your life right now, whether new friend or old acquaintance. Pretend you are a piece of furniture or a pet. How would you describe yourself?

Clustering- Write the name of a room in the middle of a piece of paper. Cluster all the objects you see. Cluster the highlights of your life, the low points, or times of stress.

Dialogue- Pretend you are a policeman. Have a dialogue with your partner describing what kind of person lives in your home. Write a dialogue with an alien telling him why you own what you own.

Dreams- When you dream, do you see any of the things you own in your dream? If so, what do you think they mean?

Freewriting- Write about the most important thing in your life right now. What is your favorite possession? What do you value?

Life Snapshots- Close your eyes, see yourself making a purchase. Write about that moment. Have you had a close call and your life almost end? Write about that frozen moment in time.

Lists- Choose a room in your house and list everything in it. List your greatest intangible possessions (i.e. love, peace, hope).

Poetry- Write a poem about an heirloom in your possession. Write an ode to an item you once had but have long since discarded. Draw a picture of one of your treasures. Make a box or decorate one to hold some of your smaller items.

Road Maps- How did you accumulate all your possessions? Did you purchase them on credit, pay cash? Choose one and write a map about how you got it. Describe how you got to this economical point in your life.

Summaries- Summarize the possessions in one of your rooms. You also can look at each year of your life and take inventory of the growth you have accomplished, the baggage you've carried around, or how you've felt about each past year.

Unsent Letters- Choose a personal object. If you were to die tomorrow, to whom would you like to give the object? Write a letter to that person telling him or her why. Has there ever been something stolen from you? Write a letter to the person who took it.

Views- Do you think people can have too many possessions? What possessions do you think people need for survival and happiness? If you had to choose one possession and only one, what would it be? Why?

Money

Character Sketch- Choose a particular money denomination and write a sketch about it. If a thousand-dollar bill was a person, where would he live? What would he think of the rest of us? Write a sketch about a rich person. A poor person.

Clustering- Cluster different amounts of money and things you can buy with that amount. Use the words rich, poor, or greedy.

Dialogue- Dialogue with George Washington, Abraham Lincoln, or any other individual whose face is on money. You can dialogue with money itself, Donald Trump or Nelson Rockefeller.

Dreams- Write about a dream that included money. Do you daydream about the lack of money? Write about what is on your mind.

Freewriting- Put your thoughts down about any aspect of money. Do you like to spend it? Collect it? Does it fascinate you?

Life Snapshots- Choose one moment in time when you were content with the amount of money you had. Write about a time when you felt rich, poor, or greedy.

Lists- Make a list of bills you need to pay off, things you need to buy, or things you want to buy. Make a list of what you would do if money were no object.

Poetry- Write a poem about gold and silver, the history of money as you know it or the qualities and power it possesses. Find different coin denominations and make rubbings of them. Put one to a page; write a short poem about each.

Road Maps- Write a map on how you arrived at your current financial location. Do you wish to be somewhere else? Where were you ten years ago? Where do you intend to be financially five years from now? Write a map on how you intend to get there.

Summaries- Summarize what you would do with a million dollars. Write a paragraph or two as to how you can get out or stay out of debt. If you had fifty dollars, how would you spend it?

Unsent Letters- Write a letter to someone, asking him or her for enough money to set you up for life. Write a letter telling someone you are giving him or her a million dollars. Place limitations on how they can spend the money.

Views- Do you think people place too much importance on money? Do you think individuals must be wealthy to be happy? What do you think about the stock market? What are your views on entrepreneurs and other small business owners?

Nightmares

Character Sketch- Write a sketch of an object, creature or person who gives you nightmares. Personify your fears and write about what they look like, how they walk and talk.

Clustering- Cluster titles of scary movies, stories, or situations which might cause you to experience bad dreams or prevent you from falling asleep.

Dialogue- Have a dialogue with your fears, shadows on the walls, or strange noises that wake you in the middle of the night.

Dreams- Put down on paper your worst nightmares—falling, monsters chasing you, loved ones dying, going to school without any clothes on, or the end of the world.

Freewriting- Nightmares don't have to be dreams at night. We refer to horrible events and situations as nightmares. Write down your definition of a nightmare. How many have you experienced throughout your lifetime?

Life Snapshots- Write about a moment when you felt your heart leaping in your chest from fear or a dread you faced when you returned to a project or place.

Lists- Make a list of areas in your life you consider to be nightmarish. Are you involved in projects that have become nightmares? List them. What kinds of things haunt you at every corner?

Poetry- Take the word, "nightmare" and write an acrostic. In the vein of Edgar Allen Poe, write a dark poem about your fears or things that go bump in your bedroom.

Road Maps- Choose a particular fear and write a map about how this came to haunt you. If you are afraid of the dark, when did it first scare you? If you are afraid of spiders, enclosed spaces, or failure, write how you became conditioned to fear these things.

Summaries- Choose a fear and summarize the effect it has on you or your loved ones.

Unsent Letters- Write a letter to yourself, describing your worst fear or nightmare. Next, pretend you are a therapist. Write a letter back telling how you can overcome the fear, or speaking of the realities of your dream.

Views- Do you think certain movies give adults and children nightmares? Should they be banned? What is your view on horror movies and stories? Do you believe that everyone is afraid of something? What do you think people should do about their fears?

Outside/Inside Your Home

Character Sketch- Write a sketch about the inside or outside of your home. If your home were a person, what class would it fall into— lower, middle, upper? How would you describe the outside of your home? Write a sketch about one of your neighbors.

Clustering- Cluster items about the inside or outside of your home. Add things you would like to improve, remove, or purchase.

Dialogue- Dialogue with a plant inside your home, a tree outside, or a bug. Converse with your neighbor's dog or the postman.

Dreams- Write about the different places you like to take naps. Do you sleep in a hammock? On the living room floor? Maybe you daydream of planting a garden, or remodeling. Write about what you think.

Freewriting- Write about the reason you live where you live. What would you change about your location, neighborhood, or design of your home if you could?

Life Snapshots- Remember a time when you stepped outside. Freeze the time and write about that moment. Was the sun warm on your face? Was it raining? Cold? Windy? Write about a time when you noticed the silence of your home.

Lists- Make a list of what you see when you step out your front door, the back door, or look out your kitchen window. List what you would like to change about your yard or the lack of a yard. Would you like to make changes to the inside of your home?

Poetry- Write a poem with the subject and title "Home Sweet Home." Draw a picture of the inside and/or outside of your home. If you live in an apartment downtown, draw a map showing how to get to there.

Road Maps- Write a life map of how you came to find your home. Start with "I decided to move to …." Do you have a garden? Write a map of how that came to be.

Summaries- Summarize lawn work or the process of cleaning your home. Write about what you do before company comes. Summarize changes you would like to make to your home, inside or out.

Unsent Letters- Write a letter to your county commissioner regarding tax questions and road conditions, to your local sheriff about lack of or quality protection, or to a nosey neighbor.

Views- What do you think is the perfect outdoor environment? Do you think humans are overpopulating the earth and endangering wildlife?

Parents/Grandparents

Character Sketch- Write a sketch about one of your grandparents or parents.

Clustering- What do you remember about your grandparents when you were growing up? Cluster your memories of each one. You also can cluster things about your parents or experiences you had with them.

Dialogue- Dialogue with your grandparents, be they dead or alive. Converse with your parents, telling them what they did right or wrong in raising you. Pretend you are your parent, asking questions from that point of view.

Dreams- Write dreams you have had of your parents or grandparents.

Freewriting- Do you remember your grandparents? What were their occupations? If they are deceased, do you still feel their presence? Describe things you may recall about them. Write about your parents when they were younger. What do you remember about them?

Life Snapshots- Write about a certain moment in time that you spent with one of your parents or grandparents. It could be a trip to a museum or baking cookies with Grandma.

Lists- List your parents' strengths, faults, or certain mannerisms. Write about your grandparents in a similar fashion. If they passed away before your time, list what others have told you about them.

Poetry- Write a poem about what it means to be a parent or grandparent. From a child's point of view, write a poem about a grandparent or parent.

Road Maps- Write life maps for your parents or grandparents. You may choose to write about how they chose their significant other, their work, or hobbies.

Summaries- Summarize your parents' or grandparents' lives. If you were writing their epitaph, what would it say?

Unsent Letters- Have you wanted to tell your parents they hurt you, but were afraid your words would hurt them? Write your thoughts in a letter. Are your parents or grandparents dead? Do you have unfinished business, things you'd like to say?

Views- Do you think your parents did a good job of raising you? What are your views of modern parenting? How do you feel about spanking? Do you think parents should take a more active role in the education of their children?

Reflections on Things in the Past

Character Sketch- Write a sketch about someone or something from your past. Your subject may be an old friend, teacher, lover, car, home, or toy. Pretend you are someone else and write a sketch of yourself from another viewpoint and time.

Clustering- Choose a past year of your life and cluster your thoughts, perceptions, or ideas of that time.

Dialogue- Dialogue with a person you remember from your past who is now just a fading memory. Dialogue with someone no longer available who once gave you advice.

Dreams- Write dreams you have that relate to the past. Perhaps you go to school with no shoes on or are late for class. Perhaps you've lost jobs or loves and those experiences visit you in your sleep.

Freewriting- What are some vivid recollections of your past? Have you done something you are ashamed of? Proud of? Are there people absent in your life with whom you wish you still communicated?

Life Snapshots- Write about a moment in time when you were in school, got your first job, had your first date, or drove alone.

Lists- Make a list of things you'd like to change if you could. Make a list of groups and organizations you have belonged to, things you have done on the weekends through the years, or activities you'd like to do again.

Poetry- Write a poem about some place you visited that you think of often. Make and decorate a paper airplane. Fly it across the room.

Road Maps- Write life maps of different locales you have traveled to, places you have stayed, or jobs you have held.

Summaries- Write summaries of different games you've played, foods you've eaten, or trouble you've been in. Look at times in your life and summarize what makes them different from now.

Unsent Letters- Write a letter to a friend with whom you have lost touch, a person to whom you were attracted, or a past political figure.

Views- What are your views on events in the past? President Kennedy's assassination? The Challenger explosion? World War II? The death of a family member or friend?

Relationships

Character Sketch- Write a sketch of a business partner, neighbor, lover, lost love, relative, or anyone with whom you have a relationship.

Clustering- Cluster your relationship of family, friends, business associates. You also can take an individual's name and cluster the relationship—how and where you met, what you have in common.

Dialogue- Is there someone you would like to have a relationship with? Or someone whose relationship you'd like to end? Have a dialogue from a pet's point of view.

Dreams- Write about your sexual dreams. Are they about your significant other, celebrities, or strangers? Write the ending to these dreams.

Freewriting- How do you build relationships? Is your relationship base wide or narrow? Do you have a wide mix of male and female friends or is it one-sided? Write about one.

Life Snapshots- Think about the different people you associate with. Consider activities you participate in—playing ball or drinking cappuccino—and write about a moment you shared.

Lists- List your different relationships and what is significant about them. Divide your relationships into groups such as trustworthy, loyal, fun to be around, leery of. List the people around you under these categories.

Poetry- Write a poem about your relationships using the theme, "the good, the bad, and the ugly." Take the first name of one of your friends and make an acrostic using his name. Start with a blank sheet of paper, write a person's name in the middle of the sheet, and write a poem around the name. Keep writing and circling the words until the poem resembles a coil.

Road Maps- Write a life map about how you became involved in one of your relationships. Start with "I met …."

Summaries- Summarize the relationship you have with your parents, significant other, children, friends, or acquaintances.

Unsent Letters- Write a letter to someone who has hurt you so terribly that you have not been able to recover. Write to a lost love or business associate who cheated you.

Views- What are your views on relationships? Do you think trust must be exhibited on both sides of a relationship? What is your view of the opposite sex? Of your own?

Relaxation

Character Sketch- Write a character sketch of an animal at rest. Think about people you see relaxing on the beach, asleep on a plane, or in a hammock. Write a sketch about one of them.

Clustering- Cluster different ways people or animals relax. Take different relaxation techniques and cluster people who would benefit from them.

Dialogue- Do you know a person who never gets uptight? Who always seems relaxed? Carry on a dialogue with that person. Ask what his or her secret is.

Dreams- What kind of relaxation technique will take you immediately into a dream? Which thought patterns will keep you awake? Write about a dream you've had when you've practiced counting sheep, fallen asleep after sex, or forced yourself to sleep.

Freewriting- How do you relax? What kind of activities do you enjoy? Do you allow yourself much free time to do nothing? Do you become uptight when you're not working?

Life Snapshots- Sit in a chair, close your eyes and relax. Let your mind wander. Write about that moment in time. What did you feel? What did you hear? Think?

Lists- List different ways you can relax, relaxation techniques you've heard about yet haven't tried, or activities that keep you from resting.

Poetry- Think about a peaceful, calm place. Write a poem about that location. Draw a picture of a rainbow or sunset.

Road Maps- Write a life map about situations when you have been tense and found ways to relax. Are there others whose example you follow? Write a life map on how they handle stress.

Summaries- Summarize your techniques, such as massage, yoga, athletic pursuits, business dealings, a hot cup of tea, or a chat with a friend.

Unsent Letters- Write a letter to yourself explaining why relaxation is important. Pretend you are a doctor and you're writing to a patient who is stressed out. What would you tell him or her?

Views- Do you think you live in a faster paced world than your parents? Do you think modernization contributes to the stress level? Do you consider alternative medicine and prevention a key factor in overcoming stress? Why or why not?

Spiritual Life

Character Sketch- Write a character sketch of God, the mother of Jesus, the Pope, the devil, an angel, your pastor, or a child.

Clustering- Choose one of the following words and cluster people, ideas, or images around it: love, joy, peace, patience, kindness, goodness, faithfulness, gentleness, or self-control.

Dialogue- Have a dialogue with your higher power, guardian angel, or some spiritual figure you admire and respect.

Dreams- Write down a dream which caused you to seek a higher power for an interpretation. What symbols did you see? What answers did you seek? Have you dreamed of the end of the world?

Freewriting- Have you ever seen a spirit? An angel? Do you have premonitions? Were you raised in church? Write about a spiritual experience you have had.

Life Snapshots- Have you had a near death experience or had your life flash before your eyes? Write about that moment. Write about a moment when you felt a higher power around or near you.

Lists- List your sins or virtues. If you were gatekeeper to the afterlife, who would you send where? List names and tell why you would send them one place or the other. List the Ten Commandments.

Poetry- Write a poem about love's effect on people, about your higher power, heaven, hell, the afterlife, or your beliefs.

Road Maps- Where are you in your spiritual journey? Have you changed your philosophy over the years? Write a map showing where you've been or where you are going.

Summaries- Choose one of the world's religions or one of America's denominations. Summarize as much as you know about it.

Unsent Letters- Write a letter to God or your higher power, a saint, or a mythical god like Apollo, Zeus, etc.

Views- Do you believe in an afterlife? Do you believe spirits walk among us? What is your view on the life that you've led so far?

Successes

Character Sketch- Write a sketch of someone whom you see as a success. It could be Donald Trump, Mickey Spillane, Sandra Bullock, or the local grocery owner.

Clustering- Cluster ways you can succeed in a chosen area of your life. Cluster successes.

Dialogue- Dialogue with people who are successful. Let them share their wisdom with you. Dialogue with someone you would like to see succeed. What valuable information can you offer?

Dreams- Ponder a dream which didn't seem satisfactory at its conclusion. Rewrite the ending.

Freewriting- Write the definition of success as you see it. Who and what do you see as successful? Why? If you were to write the keys to success, what would they be?

Life Snapshots- Choose one successful experience and write about it. Did you complete a project, make it to the top of a mountain, or simply get a good night's sleep? How did you feel in the moment you knew you had succeeded?

Lists- List your successes and why each is important to you. Investigate different areas of your life and find successes you may have overlooked. List even the smallest success.

Poetry- Write a poem, two to five lines, starting with "Success is ...." Draw a star in the middle of a blank sheet of paper. Above or below the star write "I am a success."

Road Maps- Write a road map about how you arrived at your successes. Some may have happened quickly. Others may have been a struggle, taking years.

Summaries- Take an objective look at each of your successes. Choose one and summarize the outcome. Was that success something you wanted or do you regret it now?

Unsent Letters- Write a letter to someone telling him or her you are offering a million dollars. Pretend you are the someone else and you are getting the million dollars. Write a letter of thanks to someone who has saved your life.

Views- What is your opinion of success? Overrated? Do you think success is important in life? If you worked on a project and after failure for more than ten years, would you keep trying to make the project a success? Why?

Technology

Character Sketch- Write a sketch of a contributor to technology, perhaps the Wright Brothers, Thomas Edison, Benjamin Franklin, or Bill Gates.

Clustering- Look around your home. Choose one of our technological wonders (computer, refrigerator, television, or videocassette recorder) and cluster the many uses for it.

Dialogue- Dialogue with a person from the past about the wonders we have now. What about dialoguing with an alien, describing our inventions?

Dreams- What sort of technology do you see in your dreams? Are there vehicles, appliances, computers? What kind of inventions do you daydream about? Have you ever said, "Somebody ought to make something that …"?

Freewriting- How has the world changed since you were a child? From medical discoveries to mechanical inventions, write about the changes you see. What is one invention that has made your life more difficult? Easier?

Life Snapshots- Choose one invention and write about a moment in time when you first interacted with it.

Lists- Make a list of recreational, educational, or necessary electrical gadgets in your home. Consider everything from light switches to hair dryers.

Poetry- Write an ode to something replaced by a modern invention. Draw a picture of each, one with crayons and the other with markers. For instance, the horse and buggy was replaced by the car, and eight-track tapes by records.

Road Maps- Write a map starting with "I replaced …," "I needed _____, so I …," or "The old _____ was wearing out so I upgraded to …."

Summaries- Choose an item in your home and summarize what it is used for, how it saves time and energy, or how you thought it would be an asset to your home, but it's turned into a liability.

Unsent Letters- Write a letter to the Better Business Bureau about something you purchased that was not what it was advertised to be. Write a letter to the patent office on a new piece of technology you have invented.

Views- In your opinion, are our modern advances good for society or bad? What rules and regulations do you think should be imposed on entrepreneurs and inventors? Do you think there should be fewer restrictions?

Things Lost/Things Found

Character Sketch- Give human-like characteristics to things like keys, shoes, socks, innocence, rage or love. Choose one and write about it. What would it look like? How would it speak? Would it speak at all?

Clustering- Choose one item you have lost in the past or lose frequently. Cluster the many places this item might be found.

Dialogue- Dialogue with someone or something you have lost or found. An example might be a friend, a lost relative, an address, or an old sweater.

Dreams- Write about finding a lost item through a dream.

Freewriting- Have you lost an item and never been able to find it? Have you lost an item only to discover it in your hand or on your head, etc.? Write about the experience.

Life Snapshots- Write about the emptiness you felt when you lost an item or the exuberance when you found something you lost.

Lists- Make a list of things you've lost that you need to search for. List places where you have stored or put certain items.

Poetry- Write a poem, rhymed or unrhymed, about loss or gain. Draw a picture with details on a sheet of paper. For example, draw your dream bedroom or a scenic view. You don't have to be an artist. Draw stick men or stick furniture, just be sure to add embellishments to both. When finished, turn the page over. Go do something else for an hour. Come back and, without looking at the first picture, recreate it. Looking at the two pictures, is there anything missing from the second?

Road Maps- Write a map about the process you go through when looking for a lost item or experiencing the loss of a friend. What steps do you take or procedures do you follow to recover?

Summaries- Summarize an event when you've lost something of great importance to you which cannot be replaced, or write about finding an old friend.

Unsent Letters- Write a letter to someone in your past with whom you've lost touch. Other possibilities are deceased loved ones, alienated relatives, or ex-spouses.

Views- Do you think organization is the key to keeping track of things? What do you think is the most frequently lost item and why? What do you think is an item that could be lost, without anyone caring, and why?

Things to Improve

Character Sketch- Write a sketch about someone who needs to improve the way he or she dresses or how he or she interacts with people.

Clustering- Choose an area in your life that needs improvement and cluster ways you can improve upon it.

Dialogue- Write a dialogue with someone who you think would benefit from a straightforward conversation. If you need to confront someone about his or her need for improvement, write the discussion here first.

Dreams- Write down a dream you've had that has helped you improve or clarify some area of your life. Perhaps another person has entered your dream, making a dramatic difference to you.

Freewriting- Write about things that need to be improved, not only in your personal life, but in the world.

Life Snapshots- Choose a time when you have improved and those around you thought the improvement was great, or when others didn't like the change in you.

Lists- Make a list of improvements you would like to make mentally, socially, spiritual, or physically.

Poetry- Write a poem about improvements. Topics can range from government to entertainment. Take a drawing or another piece of art and improve it.

Road Maps- Choose an area in your life that you have improved and write a map as to how you got there. Use the starter, "I decided to ...."

Summaries- Look at some of the most dramatic and lasting improvements in your lifetime. Choose one and write a summary about it.

Unsent Letters- Write a letter to a mentor, role model, or state senator.

Views- What do you think about the improvements our government has tried to make with Medicare, national security, or road conditions? Are these improvements? Do you think annual house repairs are important? Why or why not?

Transportation

Character Sketch- Write a sketch about a taxi driver, bus driver, or race car driver. Perhaps there are drivers who scare you when you ride with them. You can write about them, also.

Clustering- Think about how many different vehicles are on the road today. Do clusters with the different types. If you own a vehicle, cluster about its maintenance.

Dialogue- Dialogue with a driver who has frightened you, your driver's ed teacher or your "favorite" back seat driver.

Dreams- Write about a dream where a vehicle—a car, truck, bicycle, or boat—played a part. Have you ever daydreamed about a vehicle you'd like to purchase? Write about it.

Freewriting- Write about your ideal car, an ugly one, or a large vehicle (limousine, farm or military equipment).

Life Snapshots- Write about the moment you went on a solo spin in your car or on a bike. Perhaps you have been more adventurous and have taken up flying or motorcycle riding. Write about that.

Lists- Make a list of vehicles you've owned, vehicles you'd like to own, maintenance you need to do to your own vehicle, reasons why you don't own a car, or why you don't need one.

Poetry- Write a short poem about a vehicle you've owned. If you don't have a car, write about the mode of transportation you use to get around. Draw a picture of your favorite vehicle. You also can draw road signs or work on a model car.

Road Maps- Write about how you learned to drive or made that "all-important" first wheel purchase. A few wheel suggestions are bicycle, skateboard, skates, motorcycle, car, or truck.

Summaries- Summarize your transportation experiences. Have you been on a ferry, flown, ridden with a wild taxi driver, the subway, experienced a car wreck?

Unsent Letters- Write a letter to the Better Business Bureau, car manufacturer, your local department of transportation, or highway patrolman expressing transit concerns. You also can write a letter to your driver's education instructor telling him how things have changed since you got your license.

Views- What are your views on mandatory seat belt buckling, loud music blaring from teens' vehicles, speeders, or aggressive drivers? Choose one of these concerns and write your views.

Vacation

Character Sketch- Write a sketch about someone with whom you enjoyed going on vacation. Write about a person who made your vacation a nightmare.

Clustering- Put the name of a state or country in the center of a blank sheet of paper and cluster points of interest or all the reasons you'd like to visit.

Dialogue- Dialogue with the curator of a museum you visited, the grumpy host or hostess of a hotel where you stayed, or your favorite traveling companion.

Dreams- Write about a dream you've had on vacation. Have you daydreamed about traveling to a foreign land? Write about either one.

Freewriting- Start writing about a place where you have vacationed that you would like to visit again. If other thoughts enter your mind, go with the flow. You might have forgotten a magical place you need to revisit. Is there a vacation you have planned for years, but not taken? Write why you've not gone.

Life Snapshots- Remember a moment when you were on vacation, when you felt at peace, and write about that frozen space of time. Perhaps you were on the top of a mountain, sitting beside a quiet stream, or on the bustling streets of a foreign city.

Lists- List all the things you need to take when you travel or list the things you have to take care of before you leave.

Poetry- Write a poem about one of your vacation destinations, the vacation itself or someone who traveled with you. Draw a scenic picture or a place of interest you visited.

Road Maps- Write a life map about planning and going on a vacation. You can start with "We decided to visit …," or "After much planning, we started …."

Summaries- Choose one of your vacations and summarize the trip.

Unsent Letters- Write to a travel agent telling him where you'd like to go and what you'd like to see; a convincing letter explaining to your boss or significant other why you needed to go on this trip; or to a person you met who impressed you.

Views- Where do you think is the best place to vacation? Do you think children should be excluded from certain vacation destinations? Do you think a vacation helps or hinders a person under a lot of stress? Why?

Work

Character Sketch- Write a sketch of a boss or co-worker. It can be someone you admire or someone you loathe.

Clustering- Take a specific work area and cluster all the jobs involved with it. For example, construction. Some of the clustered items might be carpenter, plumber, painter, etc.

Dialogue- Dialogue with a co-worker, supervisor, or manager about why you should receive a raise. If you are in management, dialogue with someone about why he shouldn't get a raise or how his workload is going to increase.

Dreams- Write about a dream which involved your work. Did you go to work nude, get fired, or get promoted?

Freewriting- Write about what you consider the perfect work environment. Have you ever worked in such a place? You might begin with "I don't like work because ...."

Life Snapshots- Write about a moment when you went to your first interview, were accepted for your first job, were fired or let go.

Lists- List the jobs you have had, the ones you'd like to have, or the responsibilities you have had at a certain job. Make a list of the occupations you'd like to try or your qualifications for a job.

Poetry- Write a poem about one of your co-workers, what you do after a long, hard day's work, or why you work. Draw a picture of your workplace. You might want to draw a picture of your boss, hang it on the wall and throw spitballs at it.

Road Maps- Write a life map as to how you chose your occupation. You can write a map about the steps you took to interviews or for the job you currently have.

Summaries- Summarize the jobs or positions you have held. Maybe you have started your own business. Do you see areas at your present job which need improving? Summarize those areas.

Unsent Letters- Write a letter of resignation from your current job, a letter to your boss or a co-worker. You may choose to write a letter to the government and complain about all the money they hold out for taxes.

Views- Do you think the government takes too much money from people who work? Do you think rich people are favored over middle class workers? Do you think minorities receive too much assistance or too little from the government?

Extra Topics

*"In this age, which believes there is a shortcut to everything,
the greatest lesson to be learned is
that the most difficult way is, in the long run,
the easiest.*

—Henry Miller

This chapter is a list of starters. If you get stumped or are tired of working with the other topics, this chapter is designed to give you a starting point. Look down the list, choose a sentence starter and begin writing.

If I could live anywhere, I'd live ….

I'd someday like to ….

My career goal is ….

If I could change one thing from my past, I'd change ….

I remember reading ….

I'd like to _____, but I can't because ….

My favorite animal is ….

It may look impossible, but I'm going to ….

If I were a stuffed animal, I would be ….

I remember when ….

I'd like to meet _____ and tell him/her ….

If I could see _____ again, I'd ….

The best time of my life was when ….

I believe/don't believe in paranormal activity because ….

Sometimes I'd like to run away to ….

If I could star in any movie, I'd ….

It doesn't matter how long it takes; I'm going to ….

My purpose in life is ….

If I could return to high school, I'd ….

My greatest achievement is ….

I agree with _____ because ….

I'd start over if I could ….

Today is a day without ….

The things I value in life are ….

I'd like to be an example to ….

My biggest secret is ….

To be happy, I'd ….

I lost my innocence when ….

My parents always worked too hard for ….

If money wasn't needed, I'd ….

Some of my favorite people are ….

To me, success is ….

I get stressed out when ….

At this moment, I feel loved and needed because ….

One day, I will ….

In the future, I see myself ….

When I am alone, I ….

The person I'd most like to analyze is ….

I find peace in ….

I would spend more time ….

If I had confidence in myself, I'd ….

I believe in God because ….

My favorite things in life are ….

The thing I find most frustrating is ….

A friend is ….

If I died tomorrow, I'd like my epitaph to read ….

I like (words, numbers, or symbols) best because ….

My favorite movie is ….

Children are ….

If we eliminate _____, we will ….

Recommended Reading

*"Author: A fool who, not content with having bored
those who lived with
him, insists on tormenting generations to come.*
—Montesquieu

Reeves, Judy. <u>A Writer's Book of Days.</u> California: New World Library, 1999. ISBN: 1-57731-100-0.

Gelb, Michael J. <u>The How-to Think Like Leonardo da Vinci Workbook.</u> New York: Dell Publishing, 1999. ISBN: 0-440-50882-7.

Cameron, Julia. <u>The Vein of Gold</u>. New York: Tarcher/Putnam, 1996. ISBN: 0-87477-836-0.

Maisel, PH.D., Eric. <u>Fearless Creating.</u> New York: Tarcher/Putnam, 1995. ISBN: 0-87477-805-0.

Junker, Howard (edited by). <u>The Writer's Notebook</u>. New York: HarperCollins, 1995. ISBN: 0-06-258618-1.

Hughes, Elaine Farris. <u>Writing From the Inner Self</u>. New York: HarperCollins, 1994. ISBN: 0-06-501437-5.

Adams, M.A., Kathleen. <u>Journal to the Self</u>. New York: Warner Books, 1990. ISBN: 0-446-39038-0.

Johnson, Dan. <u>Creative Guide to Journal Writing</u>. Colorado: Gateway Publications, 1989. ISBN: 0-962304-9-7.

Klauser, Henriette Anne. <u>Writing On Both Sides of The Brain</u>. New York: HarperCollins, 1987. ISBN: 0-06-254490-X.

Goldberg, Natalie. <u>Writing Down The Bones</u>. Boston: Shambala, 1986. ISBN: 0-87773-375-9.

Ross, Elizabeth Irvin. <u>How to Write While You Sleep</u>. Ohio: Writer's Digest Books, 1985. ISBN: 0-89879-194-4.

Sher, Barbara with Annie Gottlieb. <u>Wishcraft: How to Get What You Really Want</u>. New York: Ballantine, 1979. ISBN: 0-345-34089-2.

Date _____

Technique _____   Subject _____

Mood _____   Weather _____